The 5-Minute Mindfulness Journal for Busy Moms

Written by Amanda Lynch

Illustrated by Bonnie Lemaire

Copyright ©2021 Amanda Lynch
No part of this publication may be reproduced, stored in a retrieval system, or transmitted in any form or by any means, electronic, mechanical, photocopying, recording, scanning, or otherwise, except as permitted under Sections 107 or 108 of the 1976 United States Copyright Act, without the prior written permission of the Publisher. Requests to the Author for permission should be addressed to Amanda Lynch at rethinkingresiliencyllc@gmail.com

ISBN: 978-1-7345026-5-7
LCCN: 2021900672

Cover design: Bonnie Lemaire
Editor: Candice L. Davis

To my children, may you always know that you are deeply loved. Continue to show up as your best self.

To my Humble Haven Yoga family, thank you so much for helping to make me a more mindful mama.

Dear Busy Mama,

Sit down and relax, sis. Give yourself permission to focus on your own health and well-being. The old adage is true. You can't pour from an empty cup, and we have to put our physical, emotional, and mental health first to ensure we are able to show up as our best selves.

Your child's brain rapidly develops between conception and age six. In fact, most of your child's brain development will occur in the earliest parts of life. It's never too early (or too late) to start talking to your child about the developing brain and how it works. A nutritious diet and positive experiences and relationships are crucial for healthy brain development. By reading to, playing with, and introducing mindfulness strategies to your child, you can help him or her develop healthy, brain-boosting habits that last a lifetime.

However, your child's mindfulness practice starts with **you**! I created this journal as a companion to the kid's version, "The 5-Minute Mindfulness Journal for Kids." I encourage you to work through this journal alongside your child and to model these strategies every day. On average, it takes about ten weeks of daily practice to form a new habit, and each page is equivalent to one guided activity.

Each week, you will be introduced to a new breathing tool. Take five minutes to meditate together each day. I typically do this with my girls before bedtime to help with the transition, but you can do this at any time and in any place that best suits your family.

This journal begins by introducing a bit of brain science and terminology. We begin with the **amygdala** (uh-mig-duh-luh), the brain's security guard, where "big feelings," like flight, flight, and freeze, live. Sometimes this part of our brain roars when we are scared, angry, or frustrated, or when we think we need to protect ourselves. The **prefrontal cortex**, where logical thinking and emotional regulation live, is our brain's problem solver. The mindfulness strategies in this journal are designed to boost our emotional regulation. Lastly, the **hippocampus** is our brain's memory keeper. It stores information. Toxic stress can cause our brains to not hold on to our memories. Mindfulness helps with that too!

We can "flip our lids" when we're unable to regulate our emotions. Meditation, breathing, and yoga are mindfulness tools that help kids (and parents) think before they act. These tools can help to rescue us from "getting stuck in the mud." They help us to move from a fixed mindset to a growth mindset.

For additional information, activities, and resources, check out the bestselling book, *The Mindfulness Room*, and rethinkingresiliency.com.

Mindfulness Essentials

- **BUDDY UP**-PARENTS, I ENCOURAGE YOU TO USE THIS JOURNAL TO DEVELOP YOUR OWN MINDFULNESS PRACTICE WHILE YOUR CHILD IS WORKING FROM THE KID'S VERSION. IT MAY HELP YOUR CHILD TO TALK TO YOU ABOUT THEIR EXPERIENCE, AND IT WILL ENCOURAGE CONSISTENCY IF YOU BUDDY UP WITH THEM AND SHARE YOUR DAILY JOURNAL ENTRIES.

- **JOURNAL**-AFTER YOUR CHILD COMPLETES THEIR BREATHWORK OR MEDITATION ACTIVITIES, THEY SHOULD TAKE TIME TO NOTE HOW THEY FEEL IN THEIR JOURNAL. THEY SHOULD ALSO WRITE ABOUT GOOD AND DIFFICULT MOMENTS IN THEIR DAY. I ENCOURAGE YOU TO DO THE SAME.

- **MAKE TIME TO MEDITATE**-LIFE IS BUSY! THE KEY TO BUILDING A MINDFULNESS PRACTICE IS TO MAKE IT A PRIORITY. SET ASIDE A SPECIFIC TIME TO PRACTICE. START WITH FIVE MINUTES AND GROW FROM THERE.

- **CREATE A COZY SPACE**-YOU CAN PRACTICE ANYWHERE: IN YOUR BEDROOM, IN YOUR BACKYARD, OR EVEN IN YOUR BATHROOM. TRY TO CREATE A DEDICATED SPACE IN YOUR HOME FOR MINDFULNESS.

- **BE CONSISTENT**-JUST KEEP SHOWING UP AND PRACTICING EVERY DAY! LIKE ANYTHING ELSE, THE MORE YOU PRACTICE, THE STRONGER YOUR BRAIN WILL BE.

- **BE KIND TO YOURSELF**-CONGRATULATE YOURSELF FOR SHOWING UP! REMIND YOURSELF THAT SHOWING UP IS THE FIRST STEP TO DEVELOPING A PRACTICE. YOU'RE DOING GREAT!

don't get stuck in the mud

WE ALL HAVE BIG FEELINGS
SADNESS
ANGER
FEAR
LONELINESS
FRUSTRATION

BUT WE DON'T WANT TO GET STUCK IN THOSE FEELINGS. I CALL THAT BEING STUCK IN THE MUD.

SOMETIMES OUR BRAINS TELL US TO FLIP OUR LIDS, TO BE SCARED, TO RUN AWAY, OR TO GET STUCK IN THOSE BIG FEELINGS, EVEN WHEN WE ARE SAFE.

THIS IS OUR AMYGDALA WORKING TOO HARD.

IN THIS PROFESSIOL DEVELOPMENT WORKSHOP, YOU WILL LEARN NEW TOOLS TO HELP YOU SO YOU DON'T GET STUCK IN THE MUD. THESE TOOLS WILL HELP MAKE YOUR BRAIN STRONGER.

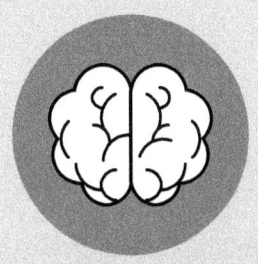

BRAIN POWER

WORDS TO KNOW

Amygdala

You have two amygdala in your brain. They are almond shaped and just above your ear. They are your brain's security guards and tell you when you are not safe. Sometimes this makes you "flip your lid". The feelings of fight, flight, and freeze are stored here.

Prefrontal cortex

Your prefrontal cortex is located in the front of your brain. It is your brain's problem solver. It helps you make good decisions, guide your behavior, and helps keep you organized.

Hippocampus

The hippocampus is located deep inside of your brain. It is your brain's memory keeper and stores information.

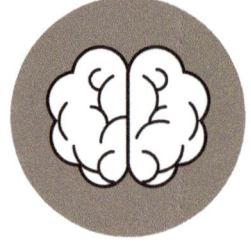

Building my amygdala toolkit

A part of building your amygdala tool kit is identifying strategies you can use when you feel "stuck in the mud."
Cut the words on this page along the dotted lines.
Then, paste them into the correct columns to create your toolkit.
You can also write in your own strategies in the boxes below.

MIND	BODY	ENVIRONMENT

✂ -

eat mindfully	drink water	recycle
plant a garden	meditate	do yoga
call a friend	listen to music	take a vacation
take a walk	unplug from the news	keep a journal
unplug from social media	read a book	set healthy boundaries

Dream big and make it

happen!

Set your intention

**CHECK THREE THINGS YOU WILL DO THIS WEEK TO BE MORE MINDFUL.
BE INTENTIONAL.**

- [ ] DRINK 8 GLASSES OF WATER A DAY
- [ ] UNPLUG FROM SOCIAL MEDIA AND THE NEWS FOR 24 HOURS
- [ ] SIT IN THE SUNSHINE
- [ ] TAKE A WALK
- [ ] CREATE A GRATITUDE JAR
- [ ] 3 MINUTES OF BELLY BREATHING
- [ ] TAKE A DANCE BREAK
- [ ] LISTEN TO YOUR FAVORITE SONG
- [ ] CALL A FRIEND
- [ ] VISIT A FAMILY MEMBER
- [ ] TAKE A BIKE RIDE
- [ ] TAKE A WARM BATH
- [ ] CUDDLE A PET
- [ ] TRY SOMETHING NEW
- [ ] READ A GOOD BOOK

Belly Breathing
Diaphragmatic breathing (3 minutes)

You are always breathing. Though your breath flows in and out it's always with you. You can control your breathing and return to it at any time. Remember you are working to make your brain stronger!

Steps
1. Get into a comfy position. You can stand, sit, or lie down. You may use a pillow, mat, cushion, or chair, just make sure you're comfortable.
2. Close your eyes if that feels okay, or you can look at the tip of your nose. Allow yourself to relax.
3. Bring your attention and awareness to your belly. As you breathe in, inflate your belly like a beach ball or balloon.
4. Relax your tummy on your exhale, when you breathe out.
5. You can also place a stuffy or doll on your belly and pretend it's riding a wave, going up and down.
6. Try this by yourself or with a buddy for three minutes.

Set Your Intention

Today I will...

- [ ] _____
- [ ] _____
- [ ] _____
- [ ] _____
- [ ] _____
- [ ] _____
- [ ] _____

Notes to Self

_____

_____

_____

_____

_____

List three things that made you happy today.

GROWING YOUR AWARENESS

During the daytime, find a quiet space outside or near a window. Take a few deep, cleansing breaths, close your eyes if you want, and bring awareness to your environment. Then, draw what you hear and smell. Come back to the same spot at night and draw what you hear and smell. Compare your drawings. Write down things that are the same and things that are different.

Day

Night

☆ ☆ SIMILARITIES ☆ ☆

_____
_____
_____

☆ ☆ DIFFERENCES ☆ ☆

_____
_____
_____

Fill YOUR JAR FIRST

LIST FIVE POSITIVE AFFIRMATIONS THAT DESCRIBE YOU.

Set Your Intention

List three things you need from others so you can be more mindful today.

Today I will...

- [ ] _____
- [ ] _____
- [ ] _____
- [ ] _____
- [ ] _____
- [ ] _____
- [ ] _____

Notes to Self

_____

_____

_____

_____

_____

WHO AM I?

Use the space below to draw a self-portrait. On the left side, draw how you look on the outside. On the right side, draw how you feel on the inside.
Don't forget to talk about it with your journal buddy if you want.
Color your creation when you're done!

Set Your Intention

What is something that frustrated you today and what did you do about it?

Today I will...

- [ ] _____
- [ ] _____
- [ ] _____
- [ ] _____
- [ ] _____
- [ ] _____
- [ ] _____

Notes to Self

_____

_____

_____

_____

_____

Focus on your
breath...

Set your intention

**CHECK THREE THINGS YOU WILL DO THIS WEEK TO BE MORE MINDFUL.
BE INTENTIONAL.**

- [ ] DRINK 8 GLASSES OF WATER A DAY
- [ ] UNPLUG FROM SOCIAL MEDIA AND THE NEWS FOR 24 HOURS
- [ ] SIT IN THE SUNSHINE
- [ ] TAKE A WALK
- [ ] CREATE A GRATITUDE JAR
- [ ] 3 MINUTES OF LION'S BREATH
- [ ] TAKE A DANCE BREAK
- [ ] LISTEN TO YOUR FAVORITE SONG
- [ ] CALL A FRIEND
- [ ] VISIT A FAMILY MEMBER
- [ ] TAKE A BIKE RIDE
- [ ] TAKE A WARM BATH
- [ ] CUDDLE A PET
- [ ] TRY SOMETHING NEW
- [ ] READ A GOOD BOOK

Lion's Breath
Simhasana
(3 minutes)

YOU ARE ALWAYS BREATHING. THOUGH YOUR BREATH FLOWS IN AND OUT IT'S ALWAYS WITH YOU. YOU CAN CONTROL YOUR BREATHING AND RETURN TO IT AT ANY TIME. REMEMBER YOU ARE WORKING TO MAKE YOUR BRAIN STRONGER!

STEPS

1. GET INTO A COMFY POSITION. I RECOMMEND SITTING ON A CUSHION, A CHAIR, OR CRISS-CROSS-APPLESAUCE ON THE FLOOR. JUST MAKE SURE YOU'RE COMFORTABLE.
2. TAKE A DEEP CLEANSING BREATH.
3. LOOK UP AT THE CEILING.
4. OPEN YOUR MOUTH AS WIDE AS YOU CAN.
5. STICK YOUR TONGUE OUT AS FAR AS IT WILL GO, CURLING YOUR TONGUE DOWNWARD.
6. EXHALE FORCEFULLY WHILE MAKING A "HAAAA" SOUND.
7. TRY THIS BY YOURSELF OR WITH A BUDDY FOR THREE MINUTES.

Set Your Intention

What is something that made you laugh today?

Today I will...

- [ ] _____
- [ ] _____
- [ ] _____
- [ ] _____
- [ ] _____
- [ ] _____
- [ ] _____

Notes to Self

_____

_____

_____

_____

_____

Fill YOUR JAR FIRST

LIST FIVE THINGS YOU ENJOY AND MAKE A COMMITMENT TO DO ONE OF THEM TODAY.

Set Your Intention

List three things that made you happy today.

Today I will...

- ☐ _____
- ☐ _____
- ☐ _____
- ☐ _____
- ☐ _____
- ☐ _____
- ☐ _____

Notes to Self

_____

_____

_____

_____

_____

_____

GROWING YOUR AWARENESS

During the daytime, find a quiet space outside or near a window. Take a few deep, cleansing breaths, close your eyes if you want, and bring awareness to your environment. Then, draw what you hear and smell. Come back to the same spot at night and draw what you hear and smell. Compare your drawings. Write down things that are the same and things that are different.

Day

Night

☆ ☆ SIMILARITIES ☆ ☆

_____
_____
_____

☆ ☆ DIFFERENCES ☆ ☆

_____
_____
_____

Set Your Intention

Today I will...

- ☐ _____
- ☐ _____
- ☐ _____
- ☐ _____
- ☐ _____
- ☐ _____
- ☐ _____

Notes to Self

_____

_____

_____

_____

_____

What are you feeling physically today?

WHAT HAPPENED THIS WEEK

Write down something you want to remember from each day.

Write a few sentences explaining why you picked those moments to remember.

Begin
within...

Set your intention

**CHECK THREE THINGS YOU WILL DO THIS WEEK TO BE MORE MINDFUL.
BE INTENTIONAL.**

- [ ] DRINK 8 GLASSES OF WATER A DAY
- [ ] UNPLUG FROM SOCIAL MEDIA AND THE NEWS FOR 24 HOURS
- [ ] SIT IN THE SUNSHINE
- [ ] TAKE A WALK
- [ ] CREATE A GRATITUDE JAR
- [ ] 3 MINUTES OF OCEAN BREATH TAKE A DANCE BREAK
- [ ] LISTEN TO YOUR FAVORITE SONG
- [ ] CALL A FRIEND
- [ ] VISIT A FAMILY MEMBER
- [ ] TAKE A BIKE RIDE
- [ ] TAKE A WARM BATH
- [ ] CUDDLE A PET
- [ ] TRY SOMETHING NEW
- [ ] READ A GOOD BOOK

Ocean breath
Ujjayi Pranayama (3 minutes)

YOU ARE ALWAYS BREATHING. THOUGH YOUR BREATH FLOWS IN AND OUT IT'S ALWAYS WITH YOU. YOU CAN CONTROL YOUR BREATHING AND RETURN TO IT AT ANY TIME. OCEAN BREATH HELPS YOU FOCUS, RELAX, AND MAKES YOUR LUNGS STRONGER.

STEPS
1. COME INTO A COMFY SEATED POSITION. THIS CAN BE IN A CHAIR, ON A MAT, OR ON A CUSHION. JUST MAKE SURE YOU ARE COMFORTABLE.
2. GRAB A MIRROR OR GLASS AND FOG IT UP WITH YOUR BREATH.
3. CALL YOUR ATTENTION TO THE HISSING SOUND THAT YOUR BREATH MAKES. IT SOUNDS SORT OF LIKE THE OCEAN. DO YOU HEAR IT?
4. CLOSE YOUR MOUTH AND SEE IF YOU CAN MAKE THE SAME SOUND AND SENSATION ON BOTH THE INHALE AND EXHALE.

THIS BREATHING PATTERN HELPS TO CALM THE BODY'S FIGHT-OR-FLIGHT RESPONSE. TRY BREATHING THIS WAY FOR THREE MINUTES.

Set Your Intention

Today I will...

- [ ] _____
- [ ] _____
- [ ] _____
- [ ] _____
- [ ] _____
- [ ] _____
- [ ] _____

Notes to Self

_____

_____

_____

_____

_____

_____

What is something that frustrated you today and what did you do about it?

Fill YOUR JAR FIRST

LIST FIVE THINGS YOU ENJOY AND MAKE A COMMITMENT TO DO ONE OF THEM TODAY.

Set Your Intention

List three things you need from others so you can be more mindful today.

Today I will...

- [ ] _____
- [ ] _____
- [ ] _____
- [ ] _____
- [ ] _____
- [ ] _____
- [ ] _____

Notes to Self

_____

_____

_____

_____

_____

GROWING YOUR AWARENESS

During the daytime, find a quiet space outside or near a window. Take a few deep, cleansing breaths, close your eyes if you want, and bring awareness to your environment. Then, draw what you hear and smell. Come back to the same spot at night and draw what you hear and smell. Compare your drawings. Write down things that are the same and things that are different.

Day

Night

☆ ☆ **SIMILARITIES** ☆ ☆

☆ ☆ **DIFFERENCES** ☆ ☆

What's Your Mood?

How are you feeling today? Sad? Happy? Excited? Mad? Frustrated? Joyful?

Draw a self-portrait of how you feel today on the image below.

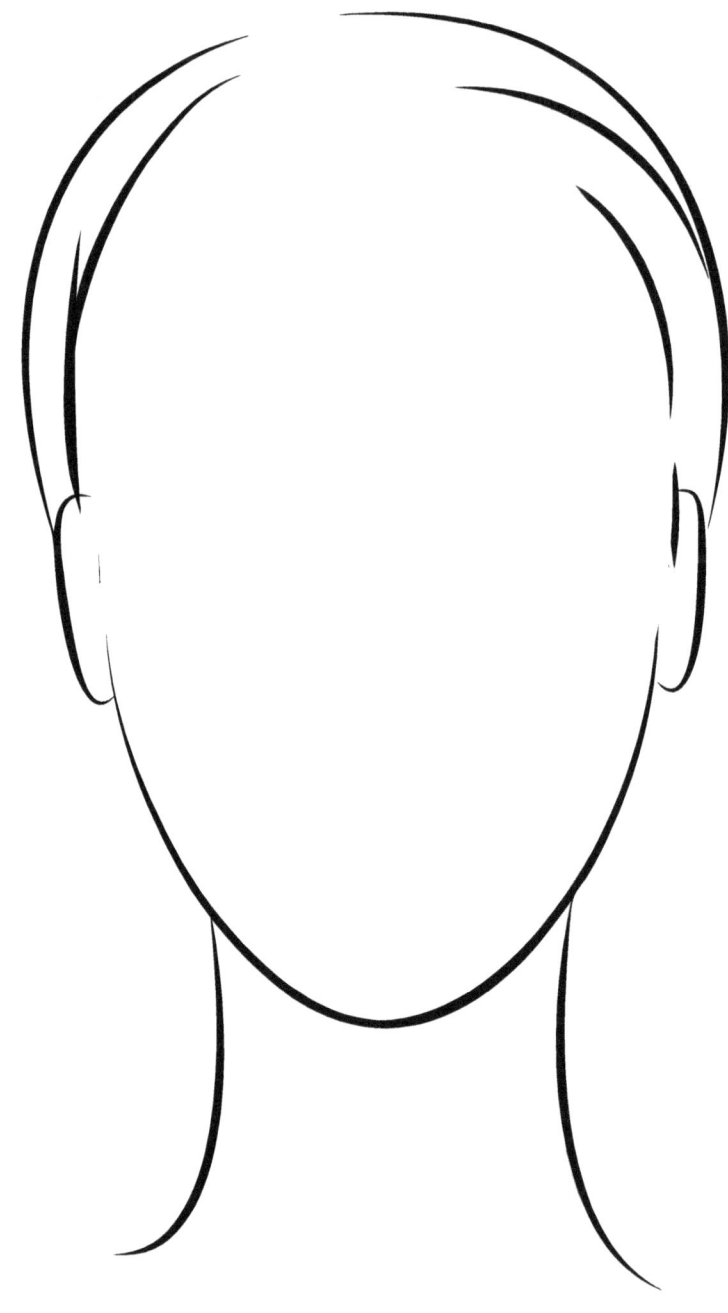

WHAT HAPPENED THIS WEEK

Write down something you want to remember from each day.

Write a few sentences explaining why you picked those moments to remember.

Set your intention

**CHECK THREE THINGS YOU WILL DO THIS WEEK TO BE MORE MINDFUL.
BE INTENTIONAL.**

- [ ] DRINK 8 GLASSES OF WATER A DAY
- [ ] UNPLUG FROM SOCIAL MEDIA AND THE NEWS FOR 24 HOURS
- [ ] SIT IN THE SUNSHINE
- [ ] TAKE A WALK
- [ ] CREATE A GRATITUDE JAR
- [ ] 3 MINUTES OF WALKING MEDITATION
- [ ] TAKE A DANCE BREAK
- [ ] LISTEN TO YOUR FAVORITE SONG
- [ ] CALL A FRIEND
- [ ] VISIT A FAMILY MEMBER
- [ ] TAKE A BIKE RIDE
- [ ] TAKE A WARM BATH
- [ ] CUDDLE A PET
- [ ] TRY SOMETHING NEW
- [ ] READ A GOOD BOOK

Dinosaur Feet
Walking Meditation
(3 minutes)

YOU ARE ALWAYS BREATHING. THOUGH YOUR BREATH FLOWS IN AND OUT IT'S ALWAYS WITH YOU. YOU CAN PRACTICE DINOSAUR FEET INSIDE OR OUTSIDE. HAVE FUN!

STEPS
1. BRING YOUR AWARENESS TO YOUR FEET.
2. CLOSE YOUR EYES AND WALK SLOWLY LEFT TO RIGHT, ROLLING YOUR ANKLES AND WIGGLING YOUR TOES.
3. SLOWLY WALK IN PLACE AND FOCUS ON THE SENSATIONS IN YOUR FEET.
4. SLOWLY LIFT YOUR FEET AND TAKE BIG STEPS ACROSS THE ROOM OR SPACE.
5. DO THIS IN SILENCE.
6. YOU CAN ALSO EXTEND OR ROLL YOUR NECK WHILE WALKING SLOWLY ACROSS THE ROOM OR SPACE.

TRY ALSO DRAWING YOUR ATTENTION TO THINGS IN YOUR ENVIRONMENT SUCH AS SOUNDS, ANIMALS, OR OTHER SENSATIONS IN YOUR BODY.

Fill YOUR JAR FIRST

FILL YOUR JAR WITH FIVE THINGS YOU ARE THANKFUL FOR TODAY.

50 AFFIRMATIONS

Circle ten statements that best describe you.
Create your own affirmation statements on the next page.

I am brave.	I am worthy.
I am happy.	I am a superstar.
I am proud.	I am dependable.
I am kind.	I am trustworthy.
I am funny.	I am amazing.
I am honest.	I am a giver.
I am thankful.	I am consistent.
I am silly.	I am capable.
I am in control of my feelings.	I am a leader.
I am smart.	I am hardworking.
I am helpful.	I am wise.
I am a good friend.	I am powerful.
I am curious.	I am open-minded.
I am resilient.	I am my own superhero.
I am talented.	I am one of a kind.
I am a problem solver.	I am perfect just the way I am.
I am a winner.	I am complete.
I am joyous.	I am quick-witted.
I am peaceful.	I am assertive.
I am safe.	I am a thinker.
I am healthy.	I am true to myself.
I am confident.	I am deserving.
I am beautiful.	I am loved.
I am strong.	I am mindful.
I am free.	I am grateful.

GROWING YOUR AWARENESS

During the daytime, find a quiet space outside or near a window. Take a few deep, cleansing breaths, close your eyes if you want, and bring awareness to your environment. Then, draw what you hear and smell. Come back to the same spot at night and draw what you hear and smell. Compare your drawings.
Write down things that are the same and things that are different.

DAY

NIGHT

SIMILARITIES

DIFFERENCES

WHAT HAPPENED THIS WEEK

Write down something you want to remember from each day.

Write a few sentences explaining why you picked those moments to remember.

I am happy.
I am kind.
I am peace.

Set your intention

**CHECK THREE THINGS YOU WILL DO THIS WEEK TO BE MORE MINDFUL.
BE INTENTIONAL.**

- [ ] DRINK 8 GLASSES OF WATER A DAY
- [ ] UNPLUG FROM SOCIAL MEDIA AND THE NEWS FOR 24 HOURS
- [ ] SIT IN THE SUNSHINE
- [ ] TAKE A WALK
- [ ] CREATE A GRATITUDE JAR
- [ ] 5-10 MINUTES OF TRATAKA MEDITATION
- [ ] TAKE A DANCE BREAK
- [ ] LISTEN TO YOUR FAVORITE SONG
- [ ] CALL A FRIEND
- [ ] VISIT A FAMILY MEMBER
- [ ] TAKE A BIKE RIDE
- [ ] TAKE A WARM BATH
- [ ] CUDDLE A PET
- [ ] TRY SOMETHING NEW
- [ ] READ A GOOD BOOK

Trataka
Candle gazing Meditation
(5-10 minutes)

YOU ARE ALWAYS BREATHING. THOUGH YOUR BREATH FLOWS IN AND OUT IT'S ALWAYS WITH YOU. CANDLE-GAZING MEDITATION HELPS TO IMPROVE YOUR CONCENTRATION AND DEEPENS YOUR RELAXTION. SIMPLY FOCUS YOUR ATTENTION ON THE FLAME OF THE CANDLE.

STEPS
1. FIND A COMFORTABLE SEAT AND LIGHT A CANDLE.
2. CLOSE YOUR EYES, SIT UP STRAIGHT, AND PLACE YOUR HANDS ON YOUR LAP.
3. FIX YOUR GAZE ON THE CANDLE'S FLAME.
4. BRING YOUR FULL ATTENTION HERE. WHAT DO YOU NOTICE?
5. DO THIS IN SILENCE. ALLOW YOURSELF TO BLINK TO AVOID EYE STRAIN.
6. BREATHE DEEPLY, OPEN YOUR EYES, AND ALLOW YOURSELF TO COME BACK INTO THE ROOM FULLY.

TRY ALSO DRAWING YOUR ATTENTION TO THE TRAILS OF SMOKE, THE COLORS OF THE FLAME, AND ANYTHING ELSE THAT YOU NOTICE.

Set Your Intention

Take a selfie. Write three positive things you notice about yourself.

Today I will...

☐ _____
☐ _____
☐ _____
☐ _____
☐ _____
☐ _____
☐ _____

Notes to Self

_____
_____
_____
_____
_____
_____

MINDFUL MOVEMENT

Stand in place and count your heartbeat for one minute.
Run in place for one minute.
Count your heartbeat again.
Do you notice a difference?
Is your heart rate faster after you run in place?
How does that make you feel?
Where do you feel different in your body?

_____
_____
_____
_____
_____
_____
_____
_____
_____

What's Your Mood?

How are you feeling today? Sad? Happy? Excited? Mad? Frustrated? Joyful?

Draw a self-portrait of how you feel today on the image below.

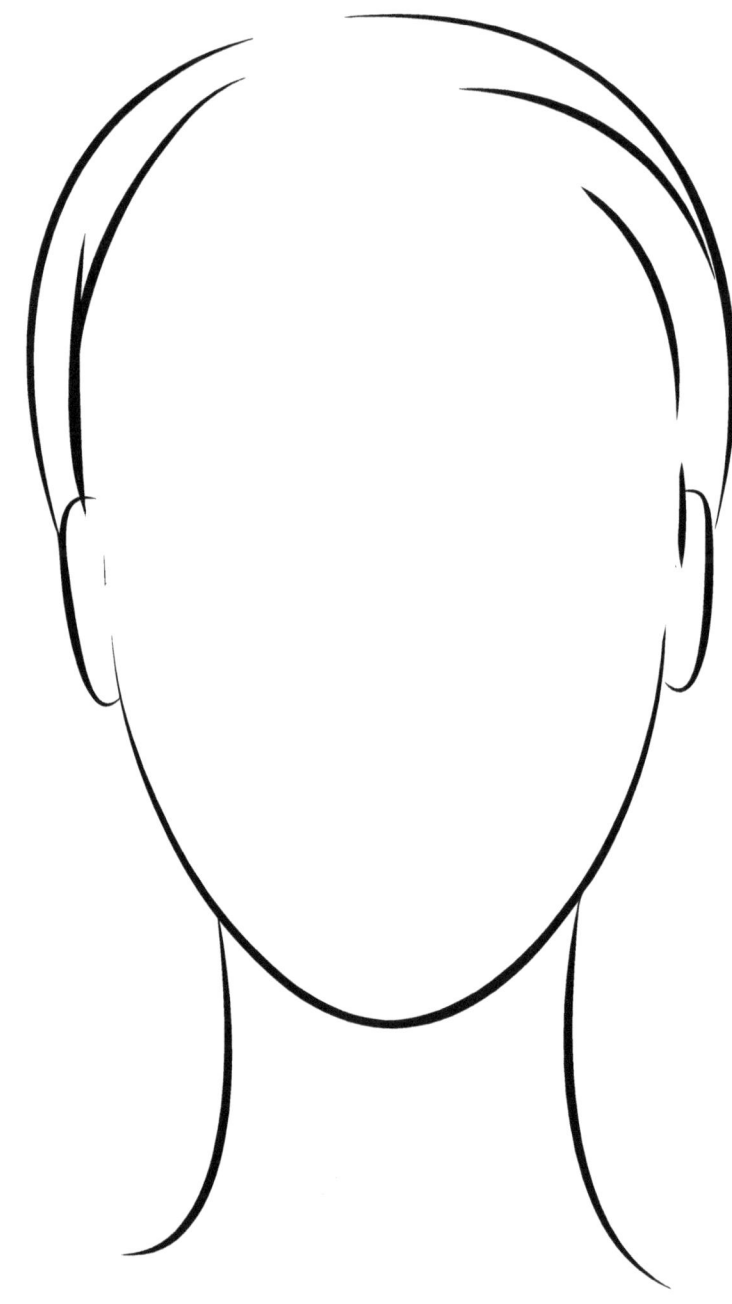

Set Your Intention

How are you celebrating yourself today?

Today I will...

- [ ] _____
- [ ] _____
- [ ] _____
- [ ] _____
- [ ] _____
- [ ] _____
- [ ] _____

Notes to Self

_____
_____
_____
_____
_____

GROWING YOUR AWARENESS

During the daytime, find a quiet space outside or near a window. Take a few deep, cleansing breaths, close your eyes if you want, and bring awareness to your environment. Then, draw what you hear and smell. Come back to the same spot at night and draw what you hear and smell. Compare your drawings.
Write down things that are the same and things that are different.

DAY

NIGHT

SIMILARITIES

_____
_____
_____
_____
_____
_____

DIFFERENCES

_____
_____
_____
_____
_____
_____

WHAT HAPPENED THIS WEEK

Write down something you want to remember from each day.

Write a few sentences explaining why you picked those moments to remember.

Set your intention

**CHECK THREE THINGS YOU WILL DO THIS WEEK TO BE MORE MINDFUL.
BE INTENTIONAL.**

- [ ] DRINK 8 GLASSES OF WATER A DAY
- [ ] UNPLUG FROM SOCIAL MEDIA AND THE NEWS FOR 24 HOURS
- [ ] SIT IN THE SUNSHINE
- [ ] TAKE A WALK
- [ ] CREATE A GRATITUDE JAR
- [ ] 3 MINUTES OF CHICKEN BREATHING
- [ ] TAKE A DANCE BREAK
- [ ] LISTEN TO YOUR FAVORITE SONG
- [ ] CALL A FRIEND
- [ ] VISIT A FAMILY MEMBER
- [ ] TAKE A BIKE RIDE
- [ ] TAKE A WARM BATH
- [ ] CUDDLE A PET
- [ ] TRY SOMETHING NEW
- [ ] READ A GOOD BOOK

Chicken Breath
Dynamic breathing
(3 minutes)

CHICKEN BREATH LOOKS RIDICULOUS, SO DON'T BE AFRAID TO LOOK SILLY! MAKE SURE YOU KEEP YOUR MOUTH CLOSED DURING THIS ACTIVITY, SO YOU WON'T BECOME DIZZY. THIS PRACTICE IS GREAT WHEN YOU NEED A QUICK BURST OF ENERGY.

STEPS
1. STAND UP AND STRETCH.
2. BEGIN TO TAKE VERY QUICK, SHORT, DEEP BREATHS IN RAPID SUCCESSION.
3. BEND YOUR ARMS AND PUMP THEM UP AND DOWN (LIKE A BELLOW) WHILE YOU BREATHE. YOUR ARMS SHOULD LOOK LIKE WINGS, BUT THEY SHOULDN'T BE LOOSE OR FLAPPY. THEY SHOULD BE STRONG.
4. YOUR ARMS SHOULD PUMP UP AS YOU INHALE AND SHOULD PUMP DOWN AS YOU EXHALE.
5. BEGIN TO BEND YOUR KNEES AS YOU EXHALE AND STRAIGHTEN YOUR KNEES AS YOU INHALE.
6. AFTER TWO MINUTES, STOP, CLOSE YOUR EYES, AND DRAW YOUR ATTENTION BACK TO YOUR BREATH.

HOW DOES YOUR BODY FEEL?

Set Your Intention

Recall a time when you helped a friend. How did that make you feel?

Today I will...

- [ ] _____
- [ ] _____
- [ ] _____
- [ ] _____
- [ ] _____
- [ ] _____
- [ ] _____

Notes to Self

_____

_____

_____

_____

_____

Fill Your Jar First

> LIST FIVE POSITIVE AFFIRMATIONS THAT DESCRIBE YOU.

Set Your Intention

What made you smile today?

Today I will...

- ☐ _____
- ☐ _____
- ☐ _____
- ☐ _____
- ☐ _____
- ☐ _____
- ☐ _____

Notes to Self

_____

_____

_____

_____

_____

GROWING YOUR AWARENESS

During the daytime, find a quiet space outside or near a window. Take a few deep, cleansing breaths, close your eyes if you want, and bring awareness to your environment. Then, draw what you hear and smell. Come back to the same spot at night and draw what you hear and smell. Compare your drawings. Write down things that are the same and things that are different.

Day	Night

☆ ☆ **SIMILARITIES** ☆ ☆

_____
_____
_____

☆ ☆ **DIFFERENCES** ☆ ☆

_____
_____
_____

Set Your Intention

What do you like best about yourself?

Today I will...

- ☐ _____
- ☐ _____
- ☐ _____
- ☐ _____
- ☐ _____
- ☐ _____
- ☐ _____

Notes to Self

_____

_____

_____

_____

_____

WHAT HAPPENED THIS WEEK

Write down something you want to remember from each day.

Write a few sentences explaining why you picked those moments to remember.

60

Show up for

yourself...

Set your intention

**CHECK THREE THINGS YOU WILL DO THIS WEEK TO BE MORE MINDFUL.
BE INTENTIONAL.**

- [ ] DRINK 8 GLASSES OF WATER A DAY
- [ ] UNPLUG FROM SOCIAL MEDIA AND THE NEWS FOR 24 HOURS
- [ ] SIT IN THE SUNSHINE
- [ ] TAKE A WALK
- [ ] CREATE A GRATITUDE JAR
- [ ] 3 MINUTES OF BODY SCAN
- [ ] TAKE A DANCE BREAK
- [ ] LISTEN TO YOUR FAVORITE SONG
- [ ] CALL A FRIEND
- [ ] VISIT A FAMILY MEMBER
- [ ] TAKE A BIKE RIDE
- [ ] TAKE A WARM BATH
- [ ] CUDDLE A PET
- [ ] TRY SOMETHING NEW
- [ ] READ A GOOD BOOK

Bedtime Body Scan
(5 minutes)

BODY SCANNING CAN HELP YOU FALL ASLEEP. THIS PRACTICE BRINGS YOUR ATTENTION AWAY FROM YOUR BREATH, AND INSTEAD FOCUSES ON BRINGING YOUR ATTENTION TO YOUR BODY.

STEPS

1. PREPARE YOURSELF FOR BED AND COME INTO A RELAXED POSITION, LYING DOWN.
2. BEGIN TO TAKE DEEP, CLEANSING, BELLY BREATHS.
3. START BY BRINGING YOUR ATTENTION TO YOUR FEET. WHAT CAN YOU PHYSICALLY FEEL IN YOUR TOES? TOP OF YOUR FOOT? ANKLE?
4. CONTINUE TO MOVE YOUR AWARENESS UP YOUR LEGS AND HIPS.
5. YOU MAY NOTICE THE TEMPERATURE OF THE AIR ON YOUR SKIN, AREAS WHERE YOUR BODY FEELS TIGHT, OR MAYBE HOW YOUR BLANKET FEELS AGAINST YOU.
6. TUNE INTO YOUR BELLY AND THEN YOUR CHEST.
7. CONTINUE TO BREATHE DEEPLY AS YOU MOVE YOUR AWARENESS THROUGH YOUR BODY.
8. MOVE YOUR AWARENESS TO YOUR FACE, TONGUE, LIPS, AND CHEEKS.
9. BRING YOUR AWARENESS TO THE CROWN OF YOUR HEAD. WHAT CAN YOU FEEL? HOW DO YOU FEEL?

Set Your Intention

What makes you happy?

Today I will...

- [ ] _____
- [ ] _____
- [ ] _____
- [ ] _____
- [ ] _____
- [ ] _____
- [ ] _____

Notes to Self

_____

_____

_____

_____

_____

What's Your Mood?

How are you feeling today? Sad? Happy? Excited? Mad? Frustrated? Joyful?

Draw a self-portrait of how you feel today on the image below.

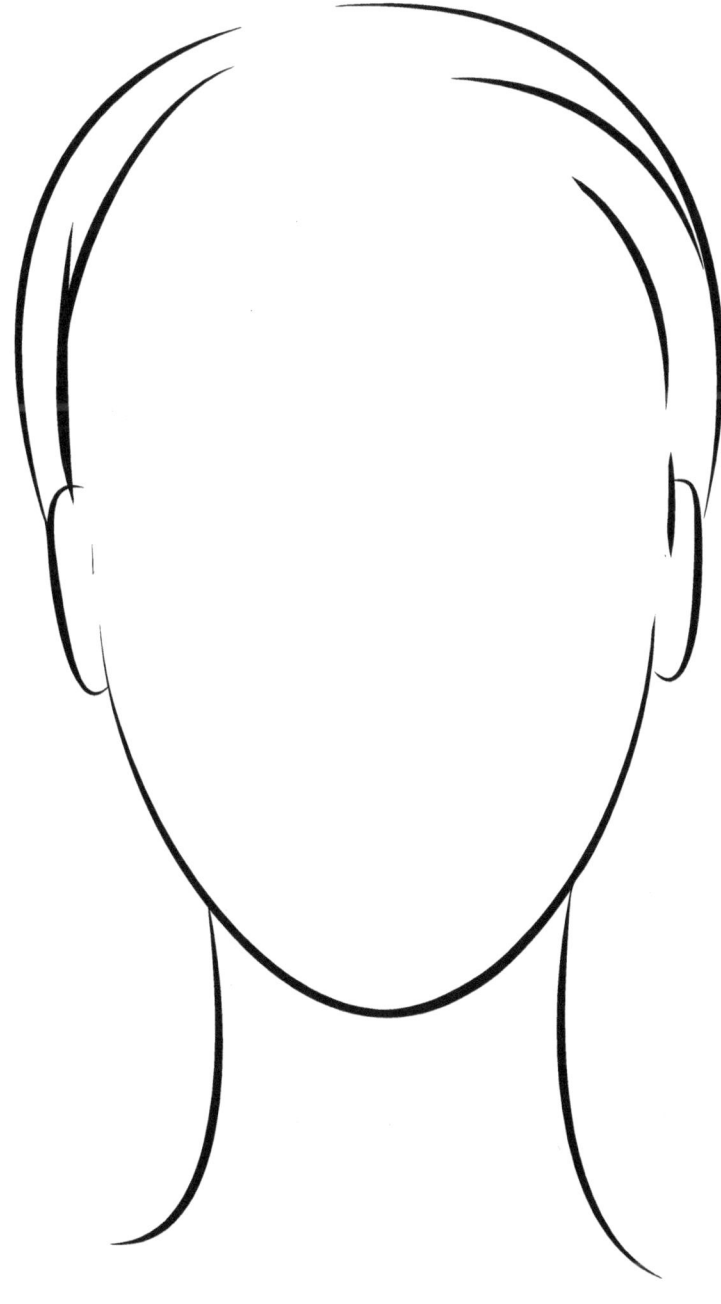

MINDFUL MOVEMENT

Put on your favorite song and take a one-minute dance break.
Take two minutes to write about how your dance break made you feel.

_____
_____
_____
_____
_____
_____
_____
_____
_____

GROWING YOUR AWARENESS

During the daytime, find a quiet space outside or near a window. Take a few deep, cleansing breaths, close your eyes if you want, and bring awareness to your environment. Then, draw what you hear and smell. Come back to the same spot at night and draw what you hear and smell. Compare your drawings.
Write down things that are the same and things that are different.

DAY

NIGHT

SIMILARITIES

DIFFERENCES

 **WHAT HAPPENED TODAY?**

Write about something that happened today that you would like you remember.

WHAT HAPPENED THIS WEEK

Write down something you want to remember from each day.

Write a few sentences explaining why you picked those moments to remember.

Set your intention

**CHECK THREE THINGS YOU WILL DO THIS WEEK TO BE MORE MINDFUL.
BE INTENTIONAL.**

- [ ] DRINK 8 GLASSES OF WATER A DAY
- [ ] UNPLUG FROM SOCIAL MEDIA AND THE NEWS FOR 24 HOURS
- [ ] SIT IN THE SUNSHINE
- [ ] TAKE A WALK
- [ ] CREATE A GRATITUDE JAR
- [ ] 3 MINUTES OF EATING MEDITATION
- [ ] TAKE A DANCE BREAK
- [ ] LISTEN TO YOUR FAVORITE SONG
- [ ] CALL A FRIEND
- [ ] VISIT A FAMILY MEMBER
- [ ] TAKE A BIKE RIDE
- [ ] TAKE A WARM BATH
- [ ] CUDDLE A PET
- [ ] TRY SOMETHING NEW
- [ ] READ A GOOD BOOK

Eating meditation (3 minutes)

DID YOU KNOW YOU CAN MEDITATE WHILE YOU EAT? GRAB A SNACK AND LET'S BRING OUR AWARENESS TO OUR FOOD. GRAPES, ORANGES, DARK CHOCOLATE, MARSHMALLOWS, PEPPERMINTS, OR LEMONS ARE GREAT FOOD CHOICES FOR THIS PRACTICE. YOU CAN EVEN USE A DRINK.

STEPS
1. GRAB A SNACK AND PLACE IT IN THE PALM OF YOUR HAND.
2. USING YOUR FIVE SENSES, MAKE OBSERVATIONS ABOUT YOUR SNACK. WHAT COLOR IS IT? WHAT DOES IT FEEL LIKE? WHAT DOES IT SMELL LIKE? WHAT TEXTURE IS IT? IS IT HOT? COLD? ROUGH? SMOOTH?
3. PLACE YOUR SNACK SLOWLY INTO YOUR MOUTH.
4. WITHOUT CHEWING, MOVE IT AROUND TO DIFFERENT AREAS OF YOUR MOUTH.
5. BEGIN TO CHEW SLOWLY. NOTE THE TASTE, SENSATION, AND TEXTURE OF YOUR FOOD.
6. SWALLOW.

WHAT DID YOU OBSERVE?

What's Your Mood?

How are you feeling today? Sad? Happy? Excited? Mad? Frustrated? Joyful?

Draw a self-portrait of how you feel today on the image below.

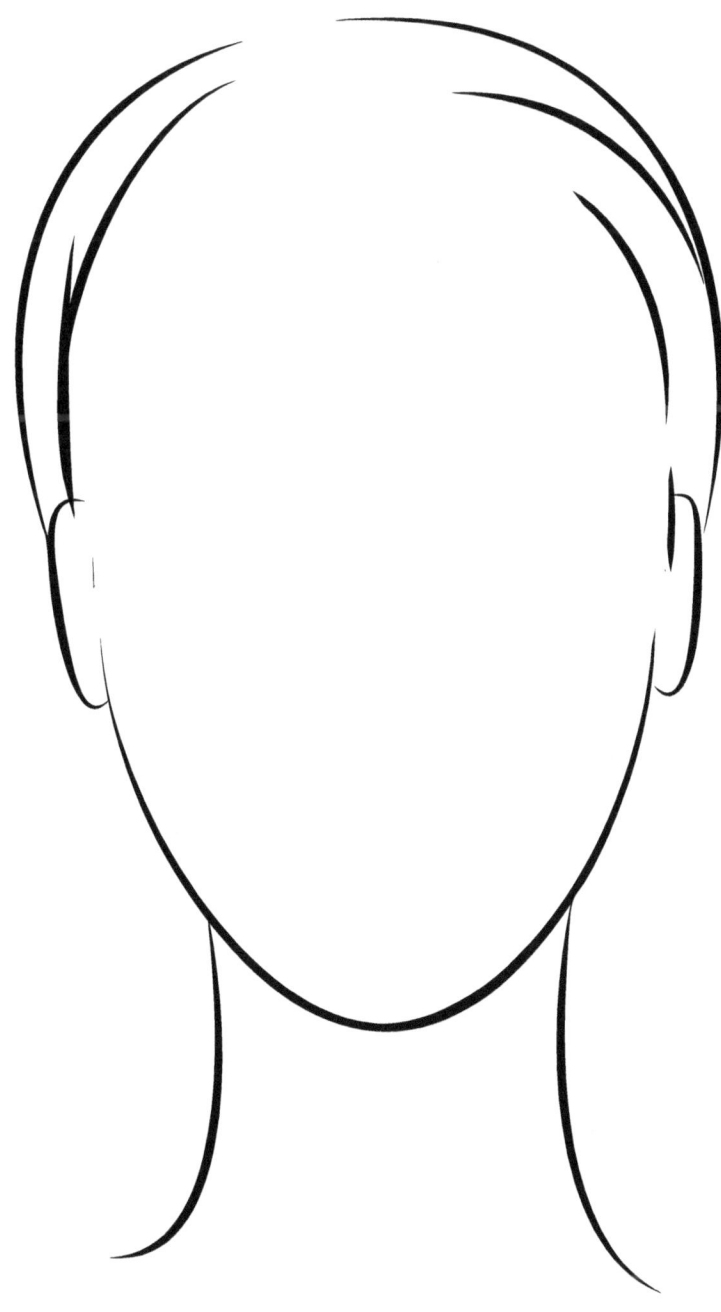

Fill YOUR JAR FIRST

> LIST THREE THINGS YOU'D DO IF YOU WEREN'T AFRAID. MAKE A PLAN TO DO ONE OF THEM THIS WEEK.

I AM....

List five affirmation statements below.

 **WHAT HAPPENED TODAY?**

Write about something that happened today that you would like you remember.

GROWING YOUR AWARENESS

During the daytime, find a quiet space outside or near a window. Take a few deep, cleansing breaths, close your eyes if you want, and bring awareness to your environment. Then, draw what you hear and smell. Come back to the same spot at night and draw what you hear and smell. Compare your drawings. Write down things that are the same and things that are different.

Day	Night

☆ ☆ SIMILARITIES ☆ ☆

_____
_____
_____

☆ ☆ DIFFERENCES ☆ ☆

_____
_____
_____

WHAT HAPPENED THIS WEEK

Write down something you want to remember from each day.

Write a few sentences explaining why you picked those moments to remember.

Listen to your *body...*

Set your intention

**CHECK THREE THINGS YOU WILL DO THIS WEEK TO BE MORE MINDFUL.
BE INTENTIONAL.**

- [ ] DRINK 8 GLASSES OF WATER A DAY
- [ ] UNPLUG FROM SOCIAL MEDIA AND THE NEWS FOR 24 HOURS
- [ ] SIT IN THE SUNSHINE
- [ ] TAKE A WALK
- [ ] CREATE A GRATITUDE JAR
- [ ] 3 MINUTES OF STILLNESS MEDITATION
- [ ] TAKE A DANCE BREAK
- [ ] LISTEN TO YOUR FAVORITE SONG
- [ ] CALL A FRIEND
- [ ] VISIT A FAMILY MEMBER
- [ ] TAKE A BIKE RIDE
- [ ] TAKE A WARM BATH
- [ ] CUDDLE A PET
- [ ] TRY SOMETHING NEW
- [ ] READ A GOOD BOOK

Stillness meditation (3 minutes)

YOU ARE ALWAYS BREATHING. THOUGH YOUR BREATH FLOWS IN AND OUT IT'S ALWAYS WITH YOU. YOU CAN CONTROL YOUR BREATHING AND RETURN TO IT AT ANYTIME. REMEMBER YOU ARE WORKING TO MAKE YOUR BRAIN STRONGER!

STEPS

1. GET INTO A COMFY POSITION. I RECOMMEND SITTING ON A CUSHION, CHAIR, OR CRISS-CROSS-APPLESAUCE ON THE FLOOR. JUST MAKE SURE YOU'RE COMFORTABLE.
2. TAKE A DEEP CLEANSING BREATH.
3. CLOSE YOUR EYES OR FIX YOUR GAZE ON THE CEILING OR THE FLOOR.
4. BRING YOUR AWARENESS TO THE NATURAL RHYTHM OF YOUR BREATH.
5. IF YOU FIND YOUR MIND WANDERING, THAT'S OKAY. JUST PICTURE THOSE THOUGHTS FLOATING AWAY LIKE THEY ARE IN A BALLOON.
6. SIMPLY RELEASE THOSE THOUGHTS AND DISTRACTIONS. LET THEM GO.
7. KEEP BREATHING NATURALLY.
8. WHEN YOU ARE READY, OPEN YOUR EYES.

WHAT ARE YOU THANKFUL FOR TODAY?

Write about three things that you are thankful for today.

What's Your Mood?

How are you feeling today? Sad? Happy? Excited? Mad? Frustrated? Joyful?

Draw a self-portrait of how you feel today on the image below.

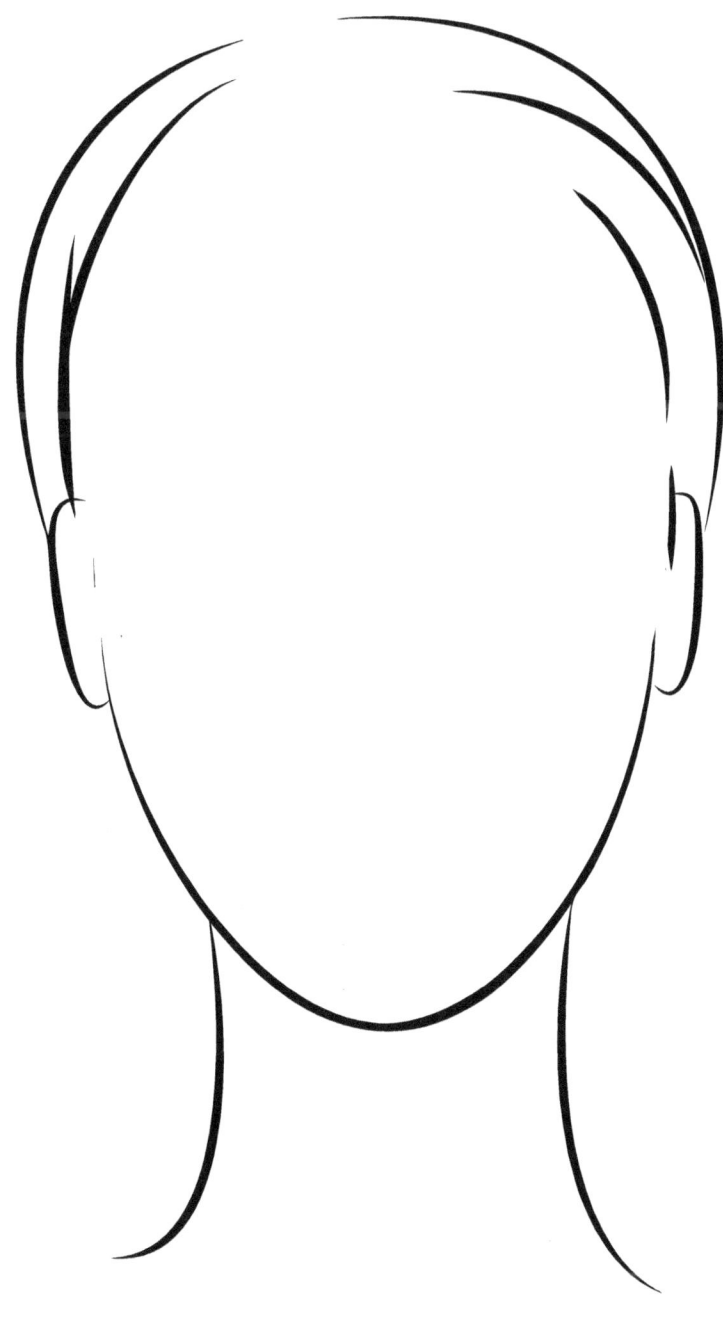

THIS OR THAT

WHAT KEEPS YOU MINDFUL?

SINGING	DANCING
MEDITATION	YOGA
COLORING	PAINTING
LONG WALKS	BICYCLE RIDES
VEGGIES	FRUIT
TALKING	LISTENING
BEING SURPRISED	STICKING TO PLANS
DAY	NIGHT

MINDFUL MOVEMENT

Put on your favorite song and take a one-minute dance break to act out the lyrics.

Take two minutes to write about how your dance break made you feel.

WHAT HAPPENED THIS WEEK

Write down something you want to remember from each day.

Write a few sentences explaining why you picked those moments to remember.

Set your intention

**CHECK THREE THINGS YOU WILL DO THIS WEEK TO BE MORE MINDFUL.
BE INTENTIONAL.**

- [ ] DRINK 8 GLASSES OF WATER A DAY
- [ ] UNPLUG FROM SOCIAL MEDIA AND THE NEWS FOR 24 HOURS
- [ ] SIT IN THE SUNSHINE
- [ ] TAKE A WALK
- [ ] CREATE A GRATITUDE JAR
- [ ] 3 MINUTES OF LABYRINTH MEDITATION
- [ ] TAKE A DANCE BREAK
- [ ] LISTEN TO YOUR FAVORITE SONG
- [ ] CALL A FRIEND
- [ ] VISIT A FAMILY MEMBER
- [ ] TAKE A BIKE RIDE
- [ ] TAKE A WARM BATH
- [ ] CUDDLE A PET
- [ ] TRY SOMETHING NEW
- [ ] READ A GOOD BOOK

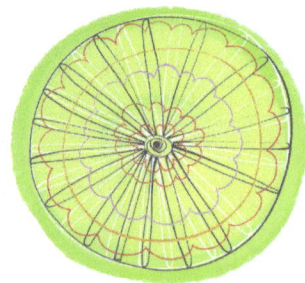

Finger Labyrinth Meditation
(3 minutes)

STEPS

1. TAKE A FEW DEEP BELLY BREATHS AND BRING YOUR ATTENTION TO THE CENTER OF THE LABYRINTH.
2. PLACE THE POINTER FINGER OF YOUR NON-DOMINANT HAND ON THE ENTRANCE AND SLOWLY TRACE THE PATTERN OF YOUR LABYRINTH.
3. FOCUS ON FOLLOWING THE PATH OF THE LABYRINTH.
4. "WALK" TO THE CENTER OF THE LABYRINTH AND REST MOMENTARILY.
5. TAKING DEEP BREATHS OBSERVING HOW YOU ARE FEELING AND RETRACE YOUR PATH OUT OF THE LABYRINTH.
6. SIT BACK, BREATHE DEEPLY AND RELAX. OBSERVE HOW YOU ARE FEELING AGAIN.

 **WHAT HAPPENED TODAY?**

Write about something that happened today that you would like you remember.

What's Your Mood?

How are you feeling today? Sad? Happy? Excited? Mad? Frustrated? Joyful?

Draw a self-portrait of how you feel today on the image below.

# **WHAT HAPPENED TODAY?**

Write about something that made you frustrated today.
What did you do about it?

MANDALA COLORING

Trust

yourself...

AUTHOR AMANDA LYNCH, MA, CTP-E, RYT-200, IS A TRAUMA INFORMED SPECIALIST WHO IS AN EXPERT IN TEACHER SELF-CARE, STUDENT AND FAMILY ENGAGEMENT, MINDFULNESS-BASED TRAUMA-INFORMED PRACTICES, AND RESTORATIVE JUSTICE.

AMANDA LIVES WITH HER HUSBAND, MARCUS, AND HER VERY BUSY CHILDREN, JUSTIN, AVA, HAZY, AND ROSEBUD, IN RICHMOND, VIRGINIA.

SHE IS THE FOUNDER OF RETHINKING RESILIENCY LLC, A THINK TANK OF PROFESSIONALS WHO PROVIDE EDUCATIONAL CONSULTING AND TRAUMA-INFORMED PROFESSIONAL DEVELOPMENT SERVICES.

ILLUSTRATOR BONNIE LEMAIRE BEGAN HER CAREER AS A FREELANCE ILLUSTRATOR WITH A PROMOTIONAL POSTCARD IN 1989. SHE IS A GRADUATE OF ONTARIO COLLEGE OF ART'S COMMUNICATION AND DESIGN PROGRAM, SPECIALIZING IN MEDICAL ILLUSTRATION. HER ETERNAL OPTIMISM IS THE FOUNDATION OF EVERY DRAWING. STILLNESS AND QUIRKY BEHAVIOR OF THOSE AROUND HER ARE A CONSTANT INSPIRATION. COMICAL AND CURIOUS CHARACTERS AND CREATURES COME ALIVE AND DANCE ON HER PAGES.

BONNIE WORKS IN HER HOME STUDIO LOCATED IN A SMALL HAMLET IN NORTHERN ONTARIO, CANADA, SURROUNDED BY HER LOVING FAMILY AND FURRY FRIEND CROWQUILL THE STUDIO CAT, NOT TO MENTION 3 QUITE LIVELY HENS CACKLING AWAY IN A CONVERTED BACKYARD TREEHOUSE CHICKEN COOP.

BOOKS SHE HAS ILLUSTRATED HAVE WON MANY AWARDS INCLUDING, FOREWORD CLARION 5-STAR-SEAL, NIEASEAL-2014-WINNER, AND NEW PINNACLE AWARD, TO NAME ONLY A FEW. BONNIE'S ECCENTRIC CREATIONS WITH FANTASTICAL STORIES HAS BROUGHT SMILES TO SMALL FACES AND DELIGHT TO HER READERS ALL OVER THE WORLD.

www.ingramcontent.com/pod-product-compliance
Lightning Source LLC
Chambersburg PA
CBHW042027100526
44587CB00029B/4326